cake.

James McIntosh
www.jamesmcintosh.co.uk

word4word

cake.

© James McIntosh

ISBN: 978-1-906316-36-5

All rights reserved. No part of this publication may be reproduced, stored in a retrieval system, or transmitted in any form, or by any means, electronic, mechanical, photocopying, recording or otherwise, without the prior permission of the publisher.

A copy of this publication has been registered with the British Library.

Published by Word4Word in 2009.

8 King Charles Court, Evesham, Worcestershire WR11 4RF

www.w4wdp.com

Printed in the UK by TJ International, Padstow.

Photography by Peter Chadwick and Ash Photography.

Designed and typeset by www.jellygraphics.co.uk and www.njlartwork.co.uk

someone left the cake out in the rain – were they mad?

I like a bit of cake. Don't we all? Homemade cakes require a bit more effort than pre-packaged ones, but they are homely. Like the rest of the books in the series, I've covered not just a basic recipe but variations too, so you can use up what is in your cupboard to prevent waste.

Next time you're shopping, have a look at the price of a cake in the store. Flour costs pence, why not make your own and even freeze some too?

As a Home Economist, I teach people how to cook and how to use domestic appliances to the best of their ability. Do you remember Home Economics in school? Well, as a profession it's about a lot more than making buns and cakes. It's about how to cook for a family on an everyday budget. It's about how to prepare food with little or no waste. It's also about producing good home-cooked food that's not complicated to make. No fiddle, no fuss, just food.

cake. is the final book in a series of four. Here I give you 46 cakes that don't cost the earth to produce, and can be made at home easily. Many of the recipes have variations as well. So in 96 pages you have over 130 recipes.

So, put the kettle on, pour yourself a cuppa and enjoy cake with me! You can find links to my YouTube and Facebook pages as well as featured recipes and lots more at www.jamesmcintosh.co.uk.

P.S. Don't forget the other books in the series
mix., dinner. and veg.

All of James's recipes are tested five times.

room temperature eggs only please

Indeed, you can't cook with a cold egg. It won't provide the oomph you need to allow the cake to rise. The human body is like an egg. Both are made of protein. If cold, limbs are not as free to move as when they're warm. It's like jumping into a cold shower. And that's what eggs are like when taken from the fridge. So if they are at room temperature, they are a lot easier to work with and will hold more air. You see, making cakes is all about the oomph: the air that you can capture in the mixture will expand in the oven and allow the cake to rise.

Baking is not that difficult, it's just a matter of care and attention. Ensure the following:

- All eggs are medium, unless said otherwise.
- All spoonfuls are flat, unless said otherwise.

cake. is small enough to keep in your handbag or manbag so you have a readymade shopping list when shopping, and comprehensive enough to bake for a family. All recipes are based on eight portions unless otherwise stated.

This is an essential cookery book for young people who want to learn how to make great everyday cakes, families interested in saving money on food bills, teachers and students of Home Economics/Food Technology and all those who love the smell of baking cake and enjoy sharing their creations with friends and family.

Contents

	Trouble shooting cakes	page 8
1	sponge – creamed mixture.	page 12
2	sponge – whisked mixture.	page 14
3	sponge – genoese.	page 16
4	sponge – all in 1.	page 17
5	victoria sandwich.	page 18
6	chocolate beetroot cake.	page 20
7	marshmallow cake.	page 22
8	cola crater cake.	page 24
9	carrot cake.	page 26
10	parkin with apples.	page 28
11	brownies.	page 30
12	caraway cake.	page 31
13	new york cheesecake.	page 32
14	chilled cheesecake.	page 34
15	rolo cake.	page 35
16	mike's red velvet cake.	page 36
17	rich fruit cake.	page 38
18	saucepan cake.	page 39
19	mexican chilli mocha cake.	page 40
20	nectarine cake.	page 42
21	madeira cake.	page 44
22	genoa cake.	page 46
23	ginger cake.	page 47
24	gateau frazier.	page 48
25	marble marshmallow spice cake with fudgy topping.	page 50
26	caramel nut cake.	page 52

27	pound cake.	page	54
28	marmalade cake.	page	55
29	chocolate fudge cake.	page	56
30	alhambra.	page	58
31	gateau pithiviers.	page	60
32	cake in a cup.	page	62
33	self saucing cake.	page	63
34	rock cakes.	page	64
35	breakfast loaf cake.	page	65
36	malt loaf.	page	66
37	pineapple upside-down cake.	page	68
38	drizzle cake.	page	70
39	angel cake.	page	71
40	gluten-free chocolate cake.	page	72
41	egg-free apple, sultana and cinnamon cake.	page	74
42	chocolate chilli polenta cake.	page	76
43	lamingtons.	page	78
44	county armagh bramley apple cake.	page	80
45	walnut and date cake.	page	82
46	cherry and almond cake.	page	84

Cake toppings

47	butter cream.	page	88
48	ganache.	page	89
49	american frosting.	page	90
50	chantilly cream.	page	91
	Index of recipes.	page	94

trouble shooting cakes

If you're a novice to baking, or just don't understand why your fruit is sinking in a cake, have a read below and hopefully you'll find the answers to your problems.

Problem	Cause
Curdling of uncooked cake mixture	A cold egg will cool the fat that surrounds it in the mixture and the fat will become surrounded by liquid from the egg, this makes emulsification of the fat by the egg yolk difficult. The mixture will hold less air. Too much egg added too quickly.
Cake has sunk in the middle	Too much sugar in the mixture causing the gluten in the flour to be over softened so that it collapses. Too much raising agent, causing the gluten to over stretch and collapse. Undercooking, caused by the wrong temperature or cooking time. Opening the oven door before the gluten has set, so the heavy cold air makes it sink. This will not occur in the Aga or Rayburn (providing the Rayburn is up to temperature).
Cake has risen to a peak and is cracked	Oven temperature is too high causing the mixture to rapidly form a peak then overcook. Too much mixture for the size of the tin. Placing the cake on too high a shelf in the oven.
Cake has a heavy texture	Too much liquid in the mixture. Too little raising agent used or incorporated during creaming or whisking. Mixture has curdled and does not hold enough air. The oven temperature is too low or the cake has not been cooked for long enough. Overbeating when adding flour, causing loss of air. Overbeating after adding liquid.

Cake has a coarse open texture	Too much raising agent has been used, causing large pockets of gas to be produced. The flour has not been mixed in sufficiently.
Cake has risen unevenly	The oven shelf is not level. The cake mixture was placed too near the source of heat, which has caused it to rise quickly on one side.
Cake has a hard sugary crust	The sugar is too coarse for the mixture and it does not dissolve in time. Too much sugar has been used.
Cake is badly shaped	The tin has been badly lined or filled with mixture. The mixture is too stiff and does not even out when baked, or is too wet and has spread out too much.
Cake is dry	Too much chemical raising agent has been used. Too little liquid has been used. Cake is overcooked.
Fruit has sunk in fruit cake	Mixture is too wet and heavy fruit cannot be held evenly throughout. The fruit is wet and therefore adds too much liquid to the cake. Too much sugar or raising agent has been used, causing the structure to collapse and the fruit to sink.

cake.

cake.

sponge – creamed mixture. sponge – whisked mixture. sponge – genoese. sponge – all in 1. victoria sandwich. chocolate beetroot cake. marshmallow cake. cola crater cake. carrot cake. parkin with apples. brownies. caraway cake. new york cheesecake. chilled cheesecake. rolo cake. mike's red velvet cake. rich fruit cake. saucepan cake. mexican chilli mocha cake. nectarine cake. madeira cake. genoa cake. ginger cake. gateau frazier. marble marshmallow spice cake with fudgy topping. caramel nut cake. pound cake. marmalade cake. chocolate fudge cake. alhambra. gateau pithiviers. cake in a cup. self saucing cake. rock cakes. breakfast loaf cake. malt loaf. pineapple upside-down cake. drizzle cake. angel cake. gluten-free chocolate cake. egg-free apple, sultana and cinnamon cake. chocolate chilli polenta cake. lamingtons. county armagh bramley apple cake. walnut and date cake. cherry and almond cake.

sponge – creamed mixture.

A general sponge.

serves 8

100g butter or margarine
100g caster sugar
2 eggs
100g self raising flour, sieved

filling
jam or cream

Here's how to make it...

- Preheat the oven to 180°C (160°C if using a fan oven) or Gas Mark 4. Grease and line 2 x 15cm sandwich tins.
- Cream the butter or margarine and sugar with a mixer or wooden spoon until the mixture is white and fluffy and drops off the spoon or mixer beater to the count of two.
- Beat the eggs together and add the eggs a little at a time to the creamed mixture. If added too quickly the mixture will curdle.
- Add the flour and mix through gently.
- Divide between the two tins and bake on the middle shelf for 20–25 minutes. When ready the sides will appear slightly shrunken from the tin and the cake will bounce back when lightly pressed.
- Turn out onto a cooling tray and leave uncovered for 10 minutes to cool.
- Sandwich together with jam, cream or other filling.

- **2 Oven Aga,** cook on the 4th set of runners in the Roasting Oven with the cold plain shelf on top for 20–25 minutes.
- **3 and 4 Oven Aga,** cook on the 4th set of runners in the Baking Oven for 20–25 minutes.
- **Rayburn,** cook on the 5th set of runners in the Main Oven with the Thermodial reading Bake for 20–25 minutes.

Variations

Chocolate Replace 1 tbsp flour with 1 tbsp cocoa.

Almond Replace 1 tbsp flour with 1 tbsp ground almonds.

Lemon Add freshly grated lemon zest to flour.

Coffee Add 1 tbsp coffee essence before adding flour.

James says...
If the mixture begins to curdle when mixing in the eggs, try adding a tablespoon of flour to the mixture.

sponge – whisked mixture.

A fatless sponge.

serves 8

5 eggs
200g caster sugar
200g self raising flour

Here's how to make it...

- Preheat the oven to 180°C (160°C if using a fan oven) or Gas Mark 4. Grease and line 2 x 20cm sandwich tins.
- Whisk the eggs and sugar together until the mixture is very light and foamy. You know the mixture is ready when you can write your name in it with the whisk and it sits for a few seconds.
- Gently fold in the flour in thirds using a metal spoon, trying to not beat any air out.
- Pour into the tins and bake for 25–30 minutes until it is set and golden. When ready the sides will appear slightly shrunken from the tin and the cake will bounce back when lightly pressed.
- 2 Oven Aga, cook on the 4th set of runners in the Roasting Oven with the cold plain shelf on top for 20–25 minutes.
- 3 and 4 Oven Aga, cook on the 4th set of runners in the Baking Oven for 20–25 minutes.
- Rayburn, cook on the 5th set of runners in the Main Oven with the Thermodial reading Bake for 20–25 minutes.

Variations

Chocolate Replace 1 tbsp flour with 1 tbsp cocoa.

Almond Replace 1 tbsp flour with 1 tbsp ground almonds.

Lemon Add freshly grated lemon zest to flour.

Coffee Add 1 tbsp coffee essence before adding flour.

James says...

As there is no fat in this recipe it's best if either frozen or eaten within 24 hours. However, to keep the cake longer, add 1 tbsp glycerine to the flour when folding in.

sponge – genoese.

A moist sponge.

serves 8

5 eggs
200g caster sugar
200g self raising flour
20g butter, melted

Here's how to make it...

- Preheat the oven to 180°C (160°C if using a fan oven) or Gas Mark 4. Grease and line 2 x 20cm sandwich tins.
- Whisk the eggs and sugar together until the mixture is very light and foamy. You know the mixture is ready when you can write your name in it with the whisk and it sits for a few seconds.
- Gently fold in the flour in thirds using a metal spoon, trying to not beat any air out.
- Add the melted butter and fold through.
- Pour into the tins and bake for 25–30 minutes until the cake is set and golden. When ready the sides will appear slightly shrunken from the tin and the cake will bounce back when lightly pressed.
- **2 Oven Aga,** cook on the 4th set of runners in the Roasting Oven with the cold plain shelf on top for 20–25 minutes.
- **3 and 4 Oven Aga,** cook on the 4th set of runners in the Baking Oven for 20–25 minutes.
- **Rayburn,** cook on the 5th set of runners in the Main Oven with the Thermodial reading Bake for 20–25 minutes.

Variations

Chocolate Replace 1 tbsp flour with 1 tbsp cocoa.

Almond Replace 1 tbsp flour with 1 tbsp ground almonds.

Lemon Add freshly grated lemon zest to flour.

Coffee Add 1 tbsp coffee essence before adding flour.

James says...

The added butter in this sponge helps this cake keep for a few days in an air-tight container.

sponge – all in 1.

A quick and easy sponge.

serves 8

- 4 eggs
- 200g caster sugar
- 200g margarine, softened
- 200g self raising flour
- 1 tsp baking powder

Here's how to make it...

- Preheat the oven to 180°C (160°C if using a fan oven) or Gas Mark 4. Grease and line 2 x 20cm sandwich tins.
- Place all the ingredients into a bowl and mix with an electric mixer.
- Pour into the tins and bake for 25–30 minutes until the filling is set and golden. When ready the sides will appear slightly shrunken from the tin and the cake will bounce back when lightly pressed.
- 2 Oven Aga, cook on the 4th set of runners in the Roasting Oven with the cold plain shelf on top for 20–25 minutes.
- 3 and 4 Oven Aga, cook on the 4th set of runners in the Baking Oven for 20–25 minutes.
- Rayburn, cook on the 5th set of runners in the Main Oven with the Thermodial reading Bake for 20–25 minutes.

Variations

Chocolate Replace 1 tbsp flour with 1 tbsp cocoa.

Almond Replace 1 tbsp flour with 1 tbsp ground almonds.

Lemon Add freshly grated lemon zest to flour.

Coffee Add 1 tbsp coffee essence before adding flour.

James says...

Quick and easy to make, but it won't rise as well or be as light as a creamed or whisked sponge.

victoria sandwich.

Possibly named after Queen Victoria who is said to have enjoyed a slice with her afternoon tea. Or so the story goes…

serves 8

225g butter or margarine, softened
225g caster sugar
4 eggs
225g self raising flour
2 tsp baking powder

Filling
4 tbsp strawberry or raspberry jam, softened

Topping
2 tbsp caster sugar

Here's how to make it...

- Preheat the oven to 180°C (160°C if using a fan oven) or Gas Mark 4. Grease and line 2 x 20cm sandwich tins.
- Place all the ingredients into a bowl and mix with an electric mixer.
- Pour into the tins and bake for 25–30 minutes until it is set and golden.
- Allow to cook and spread jam over one half and place the other half on top. Sieve caster sugar over cake and serve.
- 2 Oven Aga, cook on the 4th set of runners in the Roasting Oven with the cold plain shelf on top for 20–25 minutes.
- 3 and 4 Oven Aga, cook on the 4th set of runners in the Baking Oven for 20–25 minutes.
- Rayburn, cook on the 5th set of runners in the Main Oven with the Thermodial reading Bake for 20–25 minutes.

Variations

Lemon Victoria sandwich Spread lemon curd between cakes.

Chocolate Victoria sandwich Spread ½ quantity chocolate ganache (see page 89) between cakes.

James says...

The jam will spread more easily if softened, this can be done by placing the jam in a small bowl and beating with a spoon.

chocolate beetroot cake.

A delicious moist cake, the beetroot works well with the chocolate to keep the cake moist and velvety.

serves 10-12

450g beetroot, peeled and grated
75g semi-sweet chocolate, melted
220ml sunflower oil
275g caster sugar

3 eggs
1 tsp vanilla extract
250g plain flour
2 tsp baking powder
¼ tsp salt

Here's how to make it...

- Preheat the oven to 180°C (160°C if using a fan oven) or Gas Mark 4. Line a 23cm cake tin with greaseproof paper.
- In a bowl, mix together the beetroot, chocolate and oil.
- Whisk together all the other ingredients until well combined and gently fold beetroot and chocolate mixture through.
- Bake for 30–40 minutes until the cake has risen and a skewer comes out clean when inserted.
- 2 Oven Aga, cook on the 4th set of runners in the Roasting Oven with the cold plain shelf on top for 30–40 minutes.
- 3 and 4 Oven Aga, cook on the 4th set of runners in the Baking Oven for 30–40 minutes.
- Rayburn, cook on the 5th set of runners in the Main Oven with the Thermodial reading Bake for 30–40 minutes.

Variations

Chocolate orange and beetroot cake Add 1 tbsp Cointreau to beetroot and chocolate mix.

Chocolate raspberry and beetroot cake Add 200g fresh raspberries to mixture after folding in chocolate and beetroot mix.

Mocha chocolate and beetroot cake Add 1 shot strong espresso coffee to beetroot and chocolate mix.

James says...
Although the idea of putting beetroot in a cake sounds odd, do try this recipe - it will surprise you!

marshmallow cake.

This cake has a pretty scalloped edge due to the marshmallows hidden under the icing.
Oh, and it's yummy too.

serves 8

75g butter or margarine, softened
75g caster sugar
2 eggs, lightly beaten
100g self raising flour
½ tsp baking powder

Filling
Lemon curd

Topping
1 x 200g pack round marshmallows
200g icing sugar
Squeeze of lemon juice
Boiling water to mix

Here's how to make it...

- Preheat the oven to 180°C (160°C if using a fan oven) or Gas Mark 4. Grease and line 2 x 18cm cake tins.
- Cream the butter or margarine and sugar until light and fluffy. Gradually beat in the egg a third at a time. Beat in the flour and baking powder.
- Pour into the tins and bake for 25–30 minutes until the cake is set and golden.
- While the cake is in the oven, cut the marshmallows in half and immediately the cake is baked, leave in the tin and place these cut side down over one cake. Remove the other cake from the tin, allow to cool, then cover with lemon curd.
- When cool, remove the cake with the marshmallows from the tin. Spread a little lemon curd over the top to fill any spaces between the marshmallows. Sandwich the cakes together with the marshmallow-covered cake on top.
- Make the icing by adding the lemon juice to the icing sugar and then 1 tsp of boiling water at a time to achieve a pourable consistency. Pour over the cake and allow to set.

- 2 Oven Aga, cook on the 4th set of runners in the Roasting Oven with the cold plain shelf on top for 25–30 minutes.
- 3 and 4 Oven Aga, cook on the 4th set of runners in the Baking Oven for 25–30 minutes.
- Rayburn, cook on the 5th set of runners in the Main Oven with the Thermodial reading Bake for 25–30 minutes.

Variations

Chocolate marshmallow cake Replace 2 tbsp flour with 2 tbsp cocoa. Fill with chocolate butter cream instead of lemon curd (see page 88). Top with chocolate icing made by adding 1 tsp of cocoa to the icing and leaving out the lemon curd.

James says...

It's important to leave the cake in the tin when adding the marshmallows as the heat coming from the cake will melt the marshmallows. The sides of the tin also provide support so the marshmallows won't fall off.

cola crater cake.

This is a fun cake! For adults as well as kids.

serves 8

250g self raising flour
125g caster sugar
125g soft brown sugar
3 tbsp cocoa powder
½ tsp bicarbonate of soda
250g butter, melted
250ml cola drink
2 large eggs
1 tsp vanilla essence
80g mini marshmallows

Topping
100g butter
2 tbsp cola drink
1 tbsp cocoa powder
200g icing sugar

Decoration
2 tbsp mini white marshmallows

Here's how to make it...

- Preheat the oven to 180°C (160°C if using a fan oven) or Gas Mark 4. Grease and line a 24cm spring form tin.
- Sieve all the dry ingredients together.
- Beat the butter, cola drink, eggs and vanilla together until well mixed. Add to dry ingredients and mix together gently to form a batter.
- Carefully fold in the mini marshmallows.
- Pour into the prepared tin. Bake for 30–35 minutes until a skewer comes out of the centre clean when inserted.
- Allow to cool in the tin for 15 minutes.
- To make the topping: melt the butter in a pan with the cola and just bring to the boil. Add the cocoa powder and icing sugar and beat well.
- Pour the topping over the cake, decorate with marshmallows and allow to cool completely before removing from tin.

- **2 Oven Aga,** cook on the 4th set of runners in the Roasting Oven with the cold plain shelf on top for 30–35 minutes.
- **3 and 4 Oven Aga,** cook on the 4th set of runners in the Baking Oven for 30–35 minutes.
- **Rayburn,** cook on the 5th set of runners in the Main Oven with the Thermodial reading Bake for 30–35 minutes.

Variations

Coffee cola cake Replace cocoa powder with 3 tbsp self raising flour and add 1 tbsp coffee essence to the mixture.

James says...

If bicarbonate of soda is used in a cake on its own, the cake will taste of washing powder. Not very pleasant at all. Bicarbonate of soda produces lots of carbon dioxide when heated and this helps the cake to rise. Because of the chocolate in this recipe, the taste of the bicarbonate of soda is masked. In plain cakes baking powder is used, which is a mixture of one-third baking soda (bicarbonate of soda) to two-thirds acid: cream of tartar (tartaric acid). The acid neutralises the alkaline washing powder taste so the cake tastes yummy.

carrot cake.

A modern day classic. And it's an all in 1. Whoopee do – a quick cake!

serves 10

125ml vegetable oil
2 eggs
140g light brown sugar
250g carrots, grated
150g self raising flour
½ tsp grated nutmeg
½ tsp mixed spice
½ tsp ground cinnamon
50g sultanas

50g walnut pieces

Cream cheese topping
125g cream cheese
3 tbsp icing sugar
1 tsp lemon juice

Here's how to make it...

- Preheat the oven to 180°C (160°C if using a fan oven) or Gas Mark 4. Grease and line a 1kg loaf tin.
- Place all the ingredients into a mixing bowl and combine. Place into the prepared tin.
- Bake for 45–50 minutes until the filling is set and golden, the sides have shrunk slightly from the sides of the tin and a skewer inserted into the cake comes out clean.
- Allow to cool in the tin for 15 minutes, then turn out onto a cooling tray.
- To make the topping: beat the cream cheese adding the icing sugar a little at a time until combined. Add the lemon juice and mix together.
- When the cake has cooled, spread the topping over.

- **2 Oven Aga,** cook on the 4th set of runners in the Roasting Oven with the cold plain shelf on top for 45–50 minutes.
- **3 and 4 Oven Aga,** cook on the 4th set of runners in the Baking Oven for 45–50 minutes.
- **Rayburn,** cook on the 5th set of runners in the Main Oven with the Thermodial reading Bake for 45–50 minutes.

Variations

Courgette cake Replace carrots with courgettes.

Carrot and pumpkin cake Replace 125g carrots with 125g mashed pumpkin and add 2 tsp freshly grated ginger.

James says...

An all in 1 method is great for this cake as it does not need to rise. Although an all in 1 is a quick method, air is not captured in the cake in the same way as a creaming or whisking method, therefore the cake will not rise as much and in turn won't be as light.

parkin with apples.

Originating in Yorkshire in England and traditionally eaten on bonfire night, this version is a little different and moist as it contains apple.

serves 8

- 75g brown sugar
- 75g butter or margarine
- 150g golden syrup
- 50g plain flour
- 1 tsp ground ginger
- 1 tsp bicarbonate of soda
- 150g medium oatmeal
- ½ dessert apple, peeled, cored and grated

Here's how to make it...

- Preheat the oven to 180°C (160°C if using a fan oven) or Gas Mark 4. Grease and line a 20 x 12cm Swiss roll tin.
- Gently heat the sugar, butter or margarine and syrup.
- Sieve the flour, ginger and bicarbonate of soda into a bowl, add the oatmeal and apple and mix well. Make a well in the centre.
- Add the syrup mixture into the well and mix to a batter. Pour into the prepared tin and bake for 45 minutes–1 hour. Parkin is cooked when it feels firm to the touch and has shrunk from the sides of the tin. Allow to cool in the tin, cut into squares and serve.

- 2 Oven Aga, cook on the 4th set of runners in the Roasting Oven with the cold plain shelf on top for 45 minutes–1 hour, replacing the cold plain shelf with a large roasting tray after 20 minutes.
- 3 and 4 Oven Aga, cook on the 4th set of runners in the Baking Oven for 45 minutes–1 hour.
- Rayburn, cook on the 5th set of runners in the Main Oven with the Thermodial reading Bake for 45 minutes–1 hour.

Variations

Treacle parkin Replace syrup with treacle and leave out the apple.

James says...

Black treacle is a good substitute for the molasses sugar that this recipe traditionally uses. In 2009 I was in Jamaica at the International Federation of Home Economics annual meeting. Seeing sugar production and chewing 'sugar cane' first hand taught me a lot about the products we buy in bags ready 'refined'.

brownies.

Very chocolaty!

serves 8

- 115g butter or margarine
- 200g caster sugar
- 2 eggs
- 1 tsp vanilla extract
- 2 tbsp cocoa powder
- 60g self raising flour
- ½ tsp baking powder

Here's how to make it...

- Preheat the oven to 180°C (160°C if using a fan oven) or Gas Mark 4. Grease and line a 20cm square cake tin.
- In a large pan, melt the butter or margarine and remove from the heat. Stir in the sugar, eggs and vanilla. Beat in all the other ingredients.
- Pour into the tin and bake for 25–30 minutes until a skewer when inserted comes out clean.
- 2 Oven Aga, cook on the 4th set of runners in the Roasting Oven with the cold plain shelf on top for 25–30 minutes.
- 3 and 4 Oven Aga, cook on the 4th set of runners in the Baking Oven for 25–30 minutes.
- Rayburn, cook on the 5th set of runners in the Main Oven with the Thermodial reading Bake for 25–30 minutes.

Variations

Orange brownies Add freshly grated zest of 1 orange to mixture.

Triple chocolate brownies Add 100g milk chocolate chips and 100g white chocolate chips to mixture before baking.

Blondies Leave chocolate out of recipe.

James says...

The distinctive cracking on top of a brownie is known as the 'skudd'.

caraway cake.

A classic British tea cake, just spread a bit of butter over the top.

serves 8

- 225g plain flour
- ½ tsp baking powder
- 150g butter or margarine, softened
- 150g caster sugar
- 3 large eggs, lightly beaten
- 2 tbsp milk
- 1 tsp vanilla extract
- 3 tsp caraway seeds

Here's how to make it...

- Preheat the oven to 180°C (160°C if using a fan oven) or Gas Mark 4. Grease and line a 1kg loaf tin.
- Sieve the flour and baking powder together and set aside. Cream the butter or margarine and sugar together until light and fluffy and the mixture falls off the end of a spoon to the count of two.
- Beat the eggs into the creamed mixture in thirds, gently stir in the flour. Now stir through all the other ingredients.
- Bake for 50 minutes until a skewer when inserted into the middle comes out clean.
- 2 Oven Aga, cook on the 4th set of runners in the Roasting Oven with the cold plain shelf on top for 50 minutes.
- 3 and 4 Oven Aga, cook on the 4th set of runners in the Baking Oven for 50 minutes.
- Rayburn, cook on the 5th set of runners in the Main Oven with the Thermodial reading Bake for 50 minutes.

Variations

Wholemeal caraway cake Replace plain flour with wholemeal, but don't sieve it.

James says...
Caraway is also known as 'Persian Cumin'.

new york cheesecake.

A beautifully set baked cheesecake that's incredibly easy to make.

serves 8

Crust
50g butter, melted
100g chocolate digestives, crushed

Filling
450g cream cheese, at room temperature
175g caster sugar
3 eggs, beaten
120ml sour cream
1 tsp vanilla extract

Here's how to make it...

- Preheat the oven to 180°C (160°C if using a fan oven) or Gas Mark 4. Grease a 20cm deep spring form cake tin.
- To make the crust, mix the digestives and butter together. Spread over base of tin and refrigerate for 20 minutes to set.
- Place the cream cheese and sugar into a bowl and mix well until blended, add the eggs in thirds and beat well to incorporate.
- Add the remaining ingredients and mix through until smooth. Pour over crust.
- Place into a deep roasting tray and pour boiling water to come half way up the cake. Bake for 25–30 minutes, then turn the oven off and leave for 30 minutes.
- **2, 3 and 4 Oven Aga,** cook on the 4th set of runners in the Roasting Oven with the cold plain shelf on top for 20 minutes then transfer to the Simmering Oven for 30 minutes.
- **Rayburn,** cook on the 5th set of runners in the Main Oven with the Thermodial reading Bake for 20 minutes, then turn the Rayburn off and leave in the oven for at least 30 minutes.

Variations

Blueberry New York cheesecake Add 200g blueberries to mixture before baking.

Strawberry New York cheesecake Add 200g chopped strawberries to mixture before baking.

Raspberry New York cheesecake Add 100g raspberries to mixture before baking.

Toffee New York cheesecake Drizzle some 'Carnation Caramel' or Dulce de leche over cake in a swirly pattern before baking.

James says...

This cake is baked in a bain marie – this stops the eggs from over-cooking. The oven is turned off so the cake cooks gently and by using this gentle heat the cheesecake should not crack.

chilled cheesecake.

Classic Sunday pudding in my native Northern Ireland.

serves 8

- 1 block lemon jelly cubes
- 225g digestive biscuits, finely crushed
- 110g butter or margarine, melted
- 75g cream cheese
- 150ml double cream
- ½ tin pears, drained

Here's how to make it...

- Dissolve the jelly cubes in 250ml boiling water.
- Mix the digestives and butter or margarine together and place into the base of a loose bottomed 20cm cake tin or flan ring. Refrigerate for 20 minutes.
- Place all the other ingredients into a liquidiser and whizz until smooth.
- When the jelly is beginning to set, fold into the liquidised mixture and pour over the digestive base. Refrigerate for 2 hours before serving.

Variations

Strawberry cheesecake Replace lemon jelly with strawberry jelly and replace pears with 100g chopped strawberries.

Raspberry cheesecake Replace lemon jelly with raspberry jelly and replace pears with 100g raspberries.

Orange cheesecake Replace lemon jelly with orange jelly and replace pears with 100g mandarin segments.

James says...

To cut this cake easily, place the knife in boiling water before cutting.

rolo cake.

A quick chocolate and caramel cake.

serves 8

Cake
100g butter or margarine
100g caster sugar
2 eggs
75g self raising flour
25g cocoa powder
1 pack rolos, chopped

Filling
1 quantity chocolate butter cream (see page 88)

Here's how to make it...

- Preheat the oven to 180°C (160°C if using a fan oven) or Gas Mark 4. Grease and line 2 x 15cm sandwich tins.
- Cream the butter or margarine and sugar with a mixer or wooden spoon until the mixture is white and fluffy and drops off the spoon or mixer beater to the count of two.
- Beat the eggs together and add them a little at a time to the creamed mixture. If added too quickly the mixture will curdle.
- Add the flour and cocoa and mix through gently. Fold in the rolos.
- Divide between the two tins and bake on the middle shelf for 20–25 minutes. When ready the sides will appear slightly shrunken from the tin and the cake will bounce back when lightly pressed.
- Turn out onto a cooling tray and leave uncovered for 10 minutes to cool.
- Sandwich together with chocolate butter cream (see page 88)
- 2 Oven Aga, cook on the 4th set of runners in the Roasting Oven with the cold plain shelf on top for 20–25 minutes.
- 3 and 4 Oven Aga, cook on the 4th set of runners in the Baking Oven for 20–25 minutes.
- Rayburn, cook on the 5th set of runners in the Main Oven with the Thermodial reading Bake for 20–25 minutes.

Variations

Rolo orange cake Add freshly grated zest of 1 orange to mixture.

James says...
The rolos melt and go gooey in the cake!

mike's red velvet cake.

On a trip to NYC I was admiring my buddy Mike's kitchen and asked if he cooked as the kitchen was 'way too tidy'. The response was, 'I make a great red velvet cake'. I had never heard of that before so Mike educated me. My main concern was that my mouth would be red from the food colouring, but that's not going to happen as the colouring is baked into the cake.

serves 8

250g self raising flour, sifted
2 tbsp cocoa powder
125g salted butter, softened
300g caster sugar
2 large eggs, lightly beaten
1 tsp vanilla extract
240ml buttermilk
2 tbsp red food colouring or cochineal
1 tsp distilled white vinegar
1 tsp baking soda

To decorate
American frosting (see page 90)
3 tbsp desiccated coconut

Here's how to make it...

- Preheat the oven to 180°C (160°C if using a fan oven) or Gas Mark 4. Butter and line 2 x 23cm round cake tins.
- Sift the flour and cocoa together, set aside.
- Cream the butter and sugar together until pale and fluffy. Add the eggs in three stages, beating well between each addition.
- Mix the vanilla, buttermilk and colouring together. With the mixer running on a low speed, add a third of the flour and cocoa mixture and a third of the buttermilk mixture alternatively until they are all combined.

- In a small cup, mix the vinegar and baking soda, allow to fizz for a moment and fold into the mixture.
- Divide the mixture between the two cake tins, bake for 25–30 minutes until a skewer inserted into the centre comes out clean. Remove from the oven, allow to cool.
- To serve, sandwich the two cakes together with frosting. Cover the top and sides with frosting and coconut.
- 2 Oven Aga, cook on the 4th set of runners in the Roasting Oven with the cold plain shelf on top for 25–30 minutes.
- 3 and 4 Oven Aga, cook on the 4th set of runners in the Baking Oven for 30 minutes.
- Rayburn, cook on the 5th set of runners in the Main Oven with the Thermodial reading Bake for 30 minutes.

Variations

Beetroot red velvet cake Replace food colouring with ½ a grated beetroot.

Devil's food cake Leave out red food colouring and use unsalted butter.

James says...

A stunning looking cake. It originates from the Southern States in the USA – and not just from Mike's kitchen! It's also important to use salted butter in this recipe as the salt 'sets' the colour in the cake.

rich fruit cake.

A special occasion cake that can also be iced for a Christmas cake.

serves many

- 250g sultanas
- 3 tbsp brandy
- 250g butter, softened
- 250g caster sugar
- 4 eggs, lightly beaten
- 250g flour
- 250g glacé cherries, chopped
- 250g glacé pineapple, chopped
- 50g preserved ginger, chopped
- 100g candied peel, chopped
- 50g walnuts, chopped
- Freshly grated zest and juice of 1 lemon

Here's how to make it...

- Steep the sultanas in the brandy overnight.
- Preheat the oven to 180°C (160°C if using a fan oven) or Gas Mark 4. Grease and line a 23cm cake tin. Wrap a double layer of brown paper around the outside and tie it in place with a piece of butcher's string.
- Cream the butter and sugar together until light and fluffy and the mix falls off the spoon to the count of two. In three goes, beat in the eggs, then add the flour.
- Add all the other ingredients to the cake and mix through.
- Pour the mixture into the prepared tin. Bake for 2½ hours until a skewer comes out clean when inserted.
- 2 Oven Aga, cook on the 4th set of runners in the Roasting Oven with the cold plain shelf on top for 30 minutes, then move to the Simmering Oven for 2 hours.
- 3 and 4 Oven Aga, cook on the 4th set of runners in the Baking Oven for 2½ hours.
- Rayburn, cook on the 5th set of runners in the Main Oven with the Thermodial reading Bake for 2½ hours.

James says...

Brown paper is wrapped around this cake to stop the sides from burning due to the long cooking time.

saucepan cake.

This very moist cake can be made easily in a cast iron casserole. Odd, but it works really well.

serves 8

- 500g mixed dried fruit
- 425g can crushed pineapple, drained
- 125g butter or margarine
- 175g soft brown sugar
- 1 tsp mixed spice
- 1 tsp ground cinnamon
- 1 tsp bicarbonate of soda
- 150g plain flour
- 150g self raising flour
- 2 medium eggs, beaten

Here's how to make it...

- Preheat the oven to 180°C (160°C if using a fan oven) or Gas Mark 4. Line a 20–24cm cast iron casserole.
- Place the fruit, pineapple, butter or margarine, sugar and spice into a mixing bowl and microwave on high for 3 minutes.
- Mix well, add all the remaining ingredients, and mix again. Place into the lined casserole.
- Bake for 1½ hours until a skewer comes out clean.
- 2 Oven Aga, cook on the 4th set of runners in the Roasting Oven with the cold plain shelf on top for 30 minutes, transfer to the Simmering Oven for 2 hours.
- 3 and 4 Oven Aga, cook on the 4th set of runners in the Baking Oven for 1½ hours.
- Rayburn, cook on the 5th set of runners in the Main Oven with the Thermodial reading Bake for 1½ hours.

Variations

Cherry cake in a saucepan Add 50g chopped glacé cherries to mixture.

Quick Dundee cake Decorate top of cake with blanched almonds.

James says...

Because cast iron produces a moist radiant heat this cake will also be very moist in texture. It also freezes well.

mexican chilli mocha cake.

Crusty top, gooey filling. Yum.

serves 8

Base
225g butter or margarine softened
100g caster sugar
300g plain flour
40g cornflour

Filling
200g plain chocolate
100g butter
1 tbsp instant coffee, dissolved in a tablespoon of boiling water
1 level tsp mild chilli powder
1–2 tsp ground cinnamon
142ml soured cream
175g dark Muscavado sugar
3 eggs, beaten

Here's how to make it...

- Preheat the oven to 180°C (160°C if using a fan oven) or Gas Mark 4.
- To make the base, cream the butter or margarine with the sugar until the mixture is light and fluffy and drops off the spoon to the count of two. Add both flours and mix through.
- Evenly place onto the base of a 24 x 24cm square or 21cm round baking dish. Bake for 10 minutes.
- To make the filling, melt all the ingredients except the eggs in a bowl over a pan of boiling water. Beat in the eggs, in three goes. Pour over the base and cook for 25 minutes until the filling is set and golden. Leave to cool for 15 minutes before serving.

- 2, 3 and 4 Oven Aga, cook on the 4th set of runners in the Roasting Oven for 25–30 minutes.
- Rayburn, cook on the 5th set of runners in the Main Oven with the Thermodial reading Roast for 25–30 minutes.

Variations

Mexican caraway mocha cake Replace chilli with 1 tbsp caraway seeds.

James says...

The base of the cake is a basic shortbread mix. Alternatively, why not crush some digestive biscuits and add some melted butter to make the base?

nectarine cake.

Fruit and cake together, delicious!

serves 10

500g nectarines, cut into eighths
20g caster sugar
225g self raising flour
1 tsp baking powder
200g butter or margarine, softened
90g caster sugar
2 eggs, beaten
Freshly grated zest and juice of 1 orange
125ml milk

Here's how to make it...

- Preheat the oven to 180°C (160°C if using a fan oven) or Gas Mark 4. Grease and line a 23cm cake tin.
- Place the nectarines into a bowl and sprinkle with the 20g of caster sugar. Set aside.
- Sift the flour and baking powder together. Set aside.
- Cream the butter or margarine and sugar together until light and fluffy and the mixture falls off a spoon to the count of two.
- Gradually add the eggs to the butter and sugar, a third at a time until combined. Add the orange zest and juice.
- Add a third of the flour, mix into the mixture, then add a third of the milk, mix through, repeat until all combined.
- Place the mixture into the cake tin with the nectarines on top.
- Bake for 1 hour until the cake has come away from the sides of the tin and a skewer when inserted comes out clean. Stand for 15 minutes in the tin before turning out onto a cooling tray.

- 2 Oven Aga, cook on the 4th set of runners in the Roasting Oven with the cold plain shelf on top for 1 hour.
- 3 and 4 Oven Aga, cook on the 4th set of runners in the Baking Oven for 1 hour.
- Rayburn, cook on the 5th set of runners in the Main Oven with the Thermodial reading Bake for 1 hour.

Variations

Plum cake Replace nectarines with plums.

Peach cake Replace nectarines with peaches.

James says...

In this recipe we sift the flour and baking powder, this does four things. It mixes them together, evenly distributes the baking powder in the cake mix, incorporates air and, of course, removes lumps.

madeira cake.

Originally served with Madeira wine, and not named after the islands. Today, we enjoy it with a cup of tea.

serves 8

150g butter or margarine, softened
150g caster sugar
3 eggs, lightly beaten
2 tbsp milk
250g plain flour
1 tbsp baking powder
Grated zest 1 lemon

Here's how to make it...

- Preheat the oven to 180°C (160°C if using a fan oven) or Gas Mark 4. Grease and line a 15cm square or 18cm round tin.
- Cream the butter or margarine and sugar together until light and fluffy and the mixture falls off the end of a spoon to the count of two. Beat in the eggs and milk a little at a time.
- Fold in the flour, baking powder and lemon zest. Pour into the prepared tin.
- Bake for 30 minutes, then drop the oven temperature to 140°C (120°C if using a fan oven), Gas Mark 3 for 1½ hours. Cool on a wire tray and serve in slices.
- 2 Oven Aga, cook on the 4th set of runners in the Roasting Oven with the cold plain shelf on top for 30 minutes and then move to the Simmering Oven for 1½ hours.
- 3 and 4 Oven Aga, cook on the 4th set of runners in the Baking Oven for 30 minutes and then move to the Simmering Oven for 1½ hours.
- Rayburn, cook on the 5th set of runners in the Main Oven with the Thermodial reading Bake for 30 minutes and then drop the temperature to Simmer for 1½ hours.

Variations

Almond Madeira Substitute 75g flour for 75g ground almonds and add 1 tsp almond essence with the egg.

Cherry Madeira Add 100g quartered glacé cherries with the flour.

Coffee and walnut Madeira Add 2 tbsp coffee essence after the eggs. Add 50g chopped walnuts with the flour.

Ginger Madeira Add 100g chopped preserved ginger with the flour.

Dundee cake Add 25g ground almonds, 100g sultanas, 75g raisins, 100g currants, 50g candied peel and 25g blanched almonds. Add all of the above, except for the blanched almonds, after adding the egg. Place almonds over the surface of the cake before baking.

James says...
Try serving warm from the oven, spread with butter. Yummy!

genoa cake.

An every day cake with a great lemon flavour.
A light fruit cake.

serves 8

- 500g butter or margarine, softened
- 500g caster sugar
- 6 eggs, lightly beaten
- 250g self raising flour
- Freshly squeezed juice and grated zest of 1 lemon
- 250g currants
- 250g sultanas
- 250g raisins
- 125g lemon peel

Topping
- 1 tbsp flaked almonds

Here's how to make it...

- Preheat the oven to 180°C (160°C if using a fan oven) or Gas Mark 4. Grease and line a 23cm cake tin.
- Cream the butter or margarine and sugar together until light and fluffy and the mixture drops off the end of a spoon to the count of two.
- Add a third of the egg, then a third of the flour until all is combined beating well between each addition.
- Add the lemon peel and fruit, mix well.
- Pour into the prepared tin and sprinkle with almonds.
- Bake for 2½ hours until the cake comes away from the sides of the tin and a skewer inserted into the middle of the cake comes out clean.
- 2 Oven Aga, cook on the 4th set of runners in the Roasting Oven with the cold plain shelf on top for 30 minutes, then transfer to the Simmering Oven for 2 hours.
- 3 and 4 Oven Aga, cook on the 4th set of runners in the Baking Oven for 2½ hours.
- Rayburn, cook on the 5th set of runners in the Main Oven with the Thermodial reading Bake for 2½ hours.

James says...

I don't believe Genoa cake has anything to do with Genoa in Italy.

ginger cake.

This is a rather famous recipe in my family. My Auntie Annie made the most wonderful ginger cake.

serves 8

150g butter or margarine, softened
150g soft light brown sugar
300g self raising flour
2 eggs, beaten
1 tsp ground allspice
1 tsp ground ginger
1 tsp baking soda
75ml buttermilk

Here's how to make it...

- Preheat the oven to 180°C (160°C if using a fan oven) or Gas Mark 4. Grease and line the inside of a 1kg loaf tin.
- Place all the ingredients into a large bowl and mix until smooth and creamy.
- Bake for 45 minutes until set and golden.
- 2 Oven Aga, cook on the 4th set of runners in the Roasting Oven with the cold plain shelf on top for 45 minutes.
- 3 and 4 Oven Aga, cook on the 4th set of runners in the Baking Oven for 45 minutes.
- Rayburn, cook on the 5th set of runners in the Main Oven with the Thermodial reading Bake for 45 minutes.

Variations

Treacle cake Add 2 tbsp treacle to the mixture.

James says...

This is an all in 1 mixture, so best start the mixer slowly!

gateau frazier.

The most amazing gateau and my favourite.
I love this cake.

serves 8

Sponge
1 x genoese sponge, made in a 23cm spring form tin, cooked and cut in half (see page 46)

Syrup
90g caster sugar
65ml water
25ml kirsch

Crème mousseline
250ml milk
1 vanilla pod
2 egg yolks
60g caster sugar
20g plain flour
20g cornflour
1 tbsp kirsch
125g unsalted butter, softened

Filling
500g strawberries, cut into pieces
50g sieved strawberry jam
100g pink marzipan

Here's how to make it...

- To make the syrup, dissolve the sugar in 65ml water in a pan over a low heat. Bring to the boil for one minute, sir in the kirsch and allow to cool. When cool, pour over sponge halves.

- Make the crème mousseline by bringing the milk and vanilla pod to the boil in a saucepan. Whisk the egg yolks and sugar until pale, stir in both flours. Strain the milk into the yolk mixture, whisking constantly and beat rapidly over a low heat until thickened. Remove from heat and allow to cool completely. Add the kirsch and gradually beat in the butter, whisking between each addition.

- Cover the cut side of each sponge half with strawberry jam. Place one half back into the spring form tin. Scatter half the strawberries over, cover with crème mousseline and add the remainder of the strawberries. Place the other sponge half on top, jam side down. Roll the marzipan into a 24cm circle and place on top of the cake. Place the cake in the fridge for 30 minutes to set. Remove from the tin and serve.

James says...

Why not make double the quantity of the crème mousseline? It's full of fat and calorie dense, but it will keep in the fridge for a few days and I have no doubt it will come in useful.

marble marshmallow spice cake with fudgy topping.

Gooey and fudgy.

serves 8

Cake
200g butter or margarine, softened
200g caster sugar
1 tsp vanilla essence
4 eggs, lightly beaten
200g self raising flour
½ tsp baking powder
100g chopped walnuts
1 tsp ground cinnamon
½ tsp ground cloves
½ tsp ground nutmeg

Coffee fudge icing
200g granulated sugar
50g butter or margarine
1 dsp coffee essence
75ml condensed milk

Filling
100g marshmallows, cut in half

Here's how to make it...

- Preheat the oven to 180°C (160°C if using a fan oven) or Gas Mark 4. Grease and line 2 x 20cm cake tins.
- Cream the butter or margarine and sugar until light and fluffy and the mixture falls off the end of a spoon to the count of two.
- Add the vanilla and beat in the eggs in three goes. Add the flour and baking powder, mix through.
- Divide the mixture in two. To one half, add the walnuts, and put into one tin, to the other add the spices and place in the other tin.
- Bake for 45 minutes until a skewer when inserted comes out clean.
- To make the fudge icing place all the ingredients into a heavy based saucepan and bring to the boil, stirring continually. Keep stirring for 10 minutes, allow to cool slightly.
- To assemble: when the cake is cool, cover one half with marshmallows and place the other half on top. Cover with fudge icing.
- 2 Oven Aga, cook on the 4th set of runners in the Roasting Oven with the cold plain shelf on top for 45 minutes.
- 3 and 4 Oven Aga, cook on the 4th set of runners in the Baking Oven for 45 minutes.
- Rayburn, cook on the 5th set of runners in the Main Oven with the Thermodial reading Bake for 45 minutes.

James says...
Instead of using condensed milk why not use some dulce de leche, available in most supermarkets, added to some whipped cream?

caramel nut cake.

Caramel and nut flavours in a cake.

serves 8

Caramel
80g soft brown sugar
3 tbsp hot water

Cake mixture
150g butter or margarine, softened
250g caster sugar
½ tsp vanilla extract
3 eggs
300g self raising flour
1½ tsp baking powder
Pinch salt
300ml milk
125g chopped walnuts

Fudge icing
300g soft brown sugar
125ml milk
25g butter or margarine
½ tsp vanilla extract

Here's how to make it...

- Preheat the oven to 180°C (160°C if using a fan oven) or Gas Mark 4. Grease and line a 23cm cake tin.
- Make the caramel by heating the brown sugar in a saucepan until melted. Stir in the hot water carefully. Set aside to cool.
- To make the cake: cream the butter or margarine and the sugar together. Add the vanilla and beat the eggs into the mixture in three stages. Next add the cooled caramel and beat into the mixture in three stages.
- Add the flour, baking powder, salt and milk. Mix through and fold in the walnuts.
- Bake for 1½ hours until the cake comes away from the sides of the tin and a skewer comes out clean when inserted.
- Turn out onto a cooling tray.
- To make the icing: place the sugar, milk and butter or margarine into a saucepan and heat gently until the sugar is dissolved. Bring to the boil, stirring continuously. The sugar is ready when a little is dropped into cold water and it forms a soft ball when moved with the fingers. Remove from the heat, add the vanilla and beat until the mixture thickens. Quickly cover the cake.

- **2 Oven Aga,** cook on the 4th set of runners in the Roasting Oven with the cold plain shelf on top for 1 hour.
- **3 and 4 Oven Aga,** cook on the 4th set of runners in the Baking Oven for 1 hour.
- **Rayburn,** cook on the 5th set of runners in the Main Oven with the Thermodial reading Bake for 1 hour.

Variations

Hazelnut caramel cake Replace walnuts with hazelnuts.

Pecan caramel cake Replace walnuts with pecan nuts.

James says...

The fudge icing on this cake is a little more complex than the fudge topping on the Chocolate Fudge cake recipe on page 56. In this recipe stages in sugar cooking are required: 'soft ball' is the first stage of caramel production and the ball should be smooth and delicate when rolled between the fingers in cold water.

pound cake.

Originally called a pound cake as it required a pound of butter, a pound of flour and a pound of sugar.

serves 4

250g self raising flour
2 tsp baking powder
250g butter or margarine, softened
200g caster sugar
4 eggs, beaten
2 tsp vanilla extract

Here's how to make it...

- Preheat the oven to 180°C (160°C if using a fan oven) or Gas Mark 4. Grease and line the inside of a 2kg loaf tin.
- Place all the ingredients into a large bowl and mix until combined.
- Pour into the tin and bake for 50–60 minutes until a skewer when inserted comes out clean.
- 2 Oven Aga, cook on the 4th set of runners in the Roasting Oven with the cold plain shelf on top for 50–60 minutes.
- 3 and 4 Oven Aga, cook on the 4th set of runners in the Baking Oven for 50–60 minutes.
- Rayburn, cook on the 5th set of runners in the Main Oven with the Thermodial reading Bake for 50–60 minutes.

Variations

Chocolate pound cake Replace 50g flour with 50g cocoa.

Citrus pound cake Add freshly grated zest of 1 orange and 1 lemon.

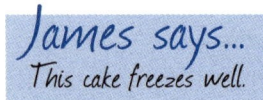

James says...
This cake freezes well.

marmalade cake.

Traditionally a Scottish recipe developed by Mrs Keiller in Dundee. Dundee is where I went to university and it was famous for jute, jam and journalism. The jam, of course, being Keiller's jam.

serves 8

- 200g self raising flour
- 100g butter or margarine, softened
- 2 eggs, beaten
- 75g caster sugar
- 2 large tbsp orange marmalade
- 1 tsp finely grated orange zest
- 2 tbsp milk

Here's how to make it...

- Preheat the oven to 180°C (160°C if using a fan oven) or Gas Mark 4. Grease and line the inside of a 18cm cake tin.
- Place the flour into a bowl and rub in the butter or margarine until the mixture resembles fine breadcrumbs.
- Stir in all the other ingredients until the mixture resembles a thick batter.
- Pour into the cake tin and bake for 1 hour until the cake is risen and golden.
- 2 Oven Aga, cook on the 4th set of runners in the Roasting Oven with the cold plain shelf on top for 1 hour.
- 3 and 4 Oven Aga, cook on the 4th set of runners in the Baking Oven for 1 hour.
- Rayburn, cook on the 5th set of runners in the Main Oven with the Thermodial reading Bake for 1 hour.

Variations

Marmalade and almond cake Add 2 tbsp ground almonds to mixture.

James says...

This cake mix is a batter. As the liquid heats in the oven the steam created will help the cake rise.

chocolate fudge cake.

Fudgy and great for a special occasion.

serves 8

Cake
110g butter
150ml vegetable oil
300ml water
300g caster sugar
100g dark chocolate
250g plain flour
3 tbsp cocoa powder
2 tsp baking powder
Pinch bicarbonate of soda
2 eggs, lightly beaten
150ml milk

Fudge Topping
75ml double cream
10g liquid glucose
125g good quality dark chocolate

Here's how to make it...

- Preheat the oven to 180°C (160°C if using a fan oven) or Gas Mark 4. Grease and line 2 x 500g loaf tins or 1 x 22cm round cake tin.
- Place the butter, oil, water, sugar and chocolate into a saucepan and bring slowly to the boil, stirring continually to dissolve the sugar. Remove from the heat.
- Sift the flour, cocoa powder, baking powder and bicarbonate of soda into a bowl. Whisk in the chocolate mixture.
- In a separate bowl, whisk together the eggs and milk and gradually whisk into the chocolate mixture.
- Pour into the lined tins, dividing the mixture between them. Place onto a baking tray and bake for about 40 minutes until the cake has come away from the sides and a skewer comes out clean when inserted. Turn out onto a cooling tray.

- To make the topping: place all ingredients into a small saucepan and stir until melted. Cool the pan until the mixture has thickened. Spread over the cake.
- 2 Oven Aga, cook on the 4th set of runners in the Roasting Oven with the cold plain shelf on top for 40 minutes.
- 3 and 4 Oven Aga, cook on the 4th set of runners in the Baking Oven for 40 minutes.
- Rayburn, cook on the 5th set of runners in the Main Oven with the Thermodial reading Bake for 40 minutes.

Variations

Chocolate cherry fudge cake Drain 1 tin of pitted black cherries and fold cherries into mixture before placing into cake tin.

Chocolate orange fudge cake Add freshly grated zest of 2 oranges and 1 tbsp Cointreau to the mixture before pouring into tin.

James says...

Liquid glucose is found in the home baking section of many supermarkets. In the USA it's known as corn syrup and is a clear sweet sticky and rather viscous liquid that comes from corn. It also stops sugar crystallising when making a syrup.

alhambra.

It's a very rich and famous chocolate cake, also known as sachertorte, named after the Sacher Hotel in Vienna, where it was first made.

serves 8

Cake
135g unsalted butter
110g caster sugar
6 egg yolks
6 egg whites
60g caster sugar
40g plain flour
40g cocoa powder
55g ground hazelnuts

Syrup
120ml water
150g sugar
1 tsp coffee extract
75ml rum

Ganache (filling)
250ml cream
250g dark chocolate, finely chopped

Glaze
150ml cream
150g dark chocolate
50g butter

Here's how to make it...

- Preheat the oven to 180°C (160°C if using a fan oven) or Gas Mark 4. Grease and line a 23cm cake tin.
- Beat the butter and sugar together until pale. Add the egg yolks gradually, beating well between additions.
- Whip the egg whites and 60g of the sugar into a stiff meringue.
- Sieve the flour and cocoa powder into a bowl and mix in the ground hazelnuts. Fold the meringue and dry ingredients alternately into the butter mixture, starting and finishing with meringue.
- Pour into the prepared tin and bake for 40 minutes or until a skewer inserted into the centre comes out clean. Turn out onto a wire rack to cool completely.
- To make the syrup: boil the water and sugar until dissolved, remove from the heat and add the coffee. Infuse for 10 minutes, add the rum, strain and reserve.
- To make the ganache: heat the cream to boiling point and pour over the finely chopped chocolate. Stir to dissolve, pour onto a flat tray and allow to set slightly before use.
- For the glaze: place all the ingredients into a pan and heat together.

- Assembly: turn the sponge upside down, trimming the top if necessary to level. Cut horizontally in half and brush both pieces with syrup to moisten.
- Spread the ganache over one of the pieces, place the second on top and press lightly to secure. Use remaining ganache to mask the sides and top of the cake. Chill.
- Place the cake onto a wire rack over a tray and pour over the glaze. Run a palette knife over the top and tap the tray to ensure it is perfectly smooth. Chill.
- Once chilled and set, remove from the wire rack, neaten the bottom edge with a knife. Place onto a cake board.
- 2 Oven Aga, cook on the 4th set of runners in the Roasting Oven with the cold plain shelf on top for 40 minutes.
- 3 and 4 Oven Aga, cook on the 4th set of runners in the Baking Oven for 40 minutes.
- Rayburn, cook on the 5th set of runners in the Main Oven with the Thermodial reading Bake for 40 minutes.

James says...

There is also a drink called an Alhambra, at time of writing I have not tried it. On a historical note, it's comprised of 1 part cognac to 5 parts hot cocoa. Make the cocoa in an Irish coffee cup and add the cognac.

gateau pithiviers.

This pastry originated in the town of Pithiviers in central France. It becomes a traditional twelfth night cake when a coin is added before the cake is sealed. The guest who gets the coin becomes king or queen for the day. During the winter holidays, these cakes can be seen adorned with gold crowns in French patisseries.

serves 4-6

Pastry
1 x 500g block puff pastry
1 egg, beaten
30g caster sugar

Filling
50g butter or margarine, softened
50g caster sugar
50g ground almonds
1 egg
½ tbsp plain flour
2 tbsp rum

Syrup
2 tbsp caster sugar
2 tbsp water

Here's how to make it...

- Preheat the oven to 200°C (180°C if using a fan oven) or Gas Mark 6.
- Cut the puff pastry in half and roll into 2 x 20cm circles.
- To make the filling, beat the butter or margarine and sugar, add the ground almonds and egg and mix well, stir in the flour and rum.
- Place one of the puff pastry circles on a baking tray, brush round the outside with beaten egg. Place the filling into the centre. Place the second piece of puff pastry on top and seal the edges using a dessert spoon handle.
- Brush the top of the pastry with beaten egg without letting any drizzle down the sides as this will stop the pastry rising.
- Bake for 25–30 minutes until the pastry is golden. Ten minutes before the end of the cooking time, remove from the oven and sprinkle with the caster sugar, return to the oven for the last 10 minutes.

- To make the syrup: mix the caster sugar with the water in a saucepan, dissolve and bring to the boil. Allow to cool slightly.
- Remove the gateau from the oven and cover with the syrup. Serve warm.
- 2, 3 and 4 Oven Aga, place the filling onto the raw pastry and cook on the floor of the Roasting Oven for 25–30 minutes.
- Rayburn, place the filling onto the raw pastry and cook on the floor of the Main Oven with the Thermodial reading Roast for 25–30 minutes.

Variations

Apple pithiviers Add 1 chopped dessert apple to the filling.

Pear pithiviers Add 1 chopped pear to the filling.

James says...

Live by my mantra. Buy pastry. It takes longer to wash up than it does to make, therefore negative time equity. Buy it, freeze it, have it to hand.

cake in a cup.

Quick and simple. I discovered this at university and it's a lot cheaper than a late night run to the shop for a chilled cake.

serves 1

25g butter or margarine, softened
25g caster sugar
½ egg
25g self raising flour
Spoonful of jam

Here's how to make it...

- Cream the butter or margarine and sugar together until light and fluffy.
- Add the egg and beat well, add the flour and mix through.
- Place the jam in the base of a microwave safe cup or mug. Place the cake mixture on top.
- Microwave on high for 2½ minutes.
- Serve.

Variations

Chocolate cake in a cup Replace 2 tsp flour with 2 tsp cocoa powder and add a few drops vanilla extract when adding the flour.

Alcoholic syrup cake in a cup Make a syrup of 1 tbsp caster sugar, 2 tsp water and 1 tsp liqueur. Bring to the boil, allow to cool a little and pour over the cake in a cup.

James says...
It's just a basic sponge really!

self saucing cake.

Comfort food on a winter's evening.

serves 8

- 175g butter or margarine, melted
- 175ml milk
- 1 tsp vanilla extract
- 1 egg, beaten
- 300g self raising flour
- 375g soft light brown sugar
- 1 tbsp cornflour
- 80g milk powder
- 300ml boiling water

Here's how to make it...

- Preheat the oven to 180°C (160°C if using a fan oven) or Gas Mark 4. Grease a 20cm cake tin.
- Whisk the butter, milk, vanilla and egg until combined.
- In a separate bowl mix together the flour and half of the sugar. Make a well in the centre and add the milk mixture. Stir to combine. Put into a cake tin.
- Mix together the remaining sugar, cornflour and milk powder. Sprinkle over the pudding. Pour the boiling water over the back of a spoon to evenly distribute the water over the cake mixture.
- Bake for 35–40 minutes until a skewer inserted into the cake comes out clean.
- 2 Oven Aga, cook on the 4th set of runners in the Roasting Oven with the cold plain shelf on top for 35–40 minutes.
- 3 and 4 Oven Aga, cook on the 4th set of runners in the Baking Oven for 35–40 minutes.
- Rayburn, cook on the 5th set of runners in the Main Oven with the Thermodial reading Bake for 35–40 minutes.

Variations

Chocolate self saucing cake Replace 50g self raising flour with 50g cocoa and the milk powder with 1 tbsp of drinking chocolate powder.

James says...

It's even easier to make this in a ceramic dish. Great for sharing.

rock cakes.

Really quick to make and great with a cuppa.

makes 8-10

- 100g self raising flour
- 50g butter or margarine, softened
- 50g caster sugar
- 50g currants or sultanas
- ½ egg, beaten

Here's how to make it...

- Preheat the oven to 200°C (180°C if using a fan oven) or Gas Mark 6.
- Sieve the flour into a bowl and rub the butter or margarine into the flour until the mixture looks like fine breadcrumbs.
- Stir through the sugar and fruit.
- Mix to a thick consistency with the beaten egg.
- Pile into 8–10 rocky heaps on a baking tray.
- Bake for 15–20 minutes until the cakes spring back when lightly pressed in the middle. Cool on a wire tray.
- **2 Oven Aga**, cook on the 4th set of runners in the Roasting Oven with the cold plain shelf on top for 15–20 minutes.
- **3 and 4 Oven Aga**, cook on the 4th set of runners in the Baking Oven for 15–20 minutes.
- **Rayburn**, cook on the 5th set of runners in the Main Oven with the Thermodial reading between Roast and Bake for 15–20 minutes.

Variations

Cherry rock cakes Replace the currants or sultanas with chopped glacé cherries.

Chocolate rock cakes Replace 1 tbsp of flour with 1 tbsp drinking chocolate.

James says...

These keep for up to four days in an airtight biscuit tin or can be frozen for up to three months.

breakfast loaf cake.

Full of flavour and fibre.

serves 8

100g butter or margarine, softened
75g light Muscavado sugar
2 medium eggs, beaten
150g dried ready to eat figs, chopped
125g wholemeal self raising flour
1 tsp mixed spice
1 tbsp golden syrup

Here's how to make it...

- Preheat the oven to 180°C (160°C if using a fan oven) or Gas Mark 4. Grease and line a 500g loaf tin.
- Cream the butter and sugar together until light and fluffy. Add the eggs and mix thoroughly.
- Mix the figs into the flour to coat evenly, fold this and all the remaining ingredients into the creamed mixture. Spoon into the tin and level the surface.
- Bake for 1 hour until the loaf comes away from the sides of the tin and a skewer when inserted comes out clean.
- 2 Oven Aga, cook on the 4th set of runners in the Roasting Oven with the cold plain shelf on top for 1 hour.
- 3 and 4 Oven Aga, cook on the 4th set of runners in the Baking Oven for 1 hour.
- Rayburn, cook on the 5th set of runners in the Main Oven with the Thermodial reading between Roast and Bake for 1 hour.

Variations

Mango figgy loaf Replace half the figs with dried mango.

James says...

If making double the mixture, in a 1kg loaf tin, add 10 minutes to the cooking time.

malt loaf.

Although not strictly a cake, this yeast bread is good for elevenses.

serves 8

1 x 7g sachet dried yeast
1 tsp caster sugar
100g wholemeal flour
100g strong white flour
½ tsp salt
100g sultanas
2 tbsp malt extract
2 tbsp treacle
25g butter or margarine
30g dark soft brown sugar
75ml hand hot water

Here's how to make it...

- Preheat the oven to 180°C (160°C if using a fan oven) or Gas Mark 4. Grease a 1kg loaf tin.
- Place the yeast, caster sugar, flour, salt and sultanas into a bowl.
- Heat the malt, treacle, butter or margarine and soft brown sugar with the water until the sugar has dissolved.
- Add this liquid to the flour and mix to a soft dough. Knead on a floured surface until no longer sticky.
- Place into the loaf tin and leave in a warm, draught-free place until doubled in size. Bake for 25–30 minutes until the loaf is golden and the bottom makes a hollow sound when tapped. Leave to cool on a wire rack.

- 2 Oven Aga, cook on the 4th set of runners in the Roasting Oven with the cold plain shelf on top for 25–30 minutes.
- 3 and 4 Oven Aga, cook on the 4th set of runners in the Baking Oven for 25–30 minutes.
- Rayburn, cook on the 5th set of runners in the Main Oven with the Thermodial reading Bake for 25–30 minutes.

Variations

Date malt loaf Add 50g chopped dates to flour mixture.

James says...

Dried yeast is sold in 7g sachets and it's a lot quicker than using fresh yeast.

pineapple upside-down cake.

A classic.

serves 8

Topping
50g butter, softened
50g light brown sugar
7 pineapple rings
7 glacé cherries

Cake
100g butter or margarine, softened
100g golden caster sugar
100g self raising flour
1 tsp baking powder
1 tsp vanilla extract
2 eggs

Here's how to make it...

- Preheat the oven to 180°C (160°C if using a fan oven) or Gas Mark 4.
- For the topping, cream the butter and sugar together until light and fluffy and spread over the base and sides of a 20cm round cake tin. Arrange the pineapple on top with a cherry in the centre of each.
- Place all the cake ingredients into a bowl and mix until smooth. Pour over the pineapple and bake for 35 minutes until golden and a skewer comes out clean when inserted.
- Turn out upside down onto a plate.
- 2 Oven Aga, cook on the 4th set of runners in the Roasting Oven with the cold plain shelf on top for 35 minutes.
- 3 and 4 Oven Aga, cook on the 4th set of runners in the Baking Oven for 35 minutes.
- Rayburn, cook on the 5th set of runners in the Main Oven with the Thermodial reading Bake for 35 minutes.

Variations

Pear upside-down cake Replace pineapple rings and cherries with tinned pear halves.

James says...
Be careful when turning out as the hot caramel round the pineapple could spill out.

drizzle cake.

Called a drizzle cake as you drizzle the icing over it.

serves 8

Cake
225g butter or margarine, softened
225g caster sugar
4 eggs, beaten
Finely grated zest of 1 lemon
225g self raising flour
2 tbsp poppy seeds

Drizzle topping
Juice of ½ lemon
100g caster sugar

Here's how to make it...

- Preheat the oven to 180°C (160°C if using a fan oven) or Gas Mark 4. Grease and line a 1kg loaf tin.
- Cream the butter and sugar together until pale and fluffy and the mixture falls off the end of a spoon to the count of two. Add the eggs in three goes, beating well. Add the lemon, flour and poppy seeds and mix well.
- Pour into the tin and bake for 45–50 minutes until a skewer when inserted comes out clean.
- Mix the sugar and lemon juice for the topping together. When the cake is still hot, poke holes all over and drizzle the topping over it.
- **2 Oven Aga,** cook on the 4th set of runners in the Roasting Oven with the cold plain shelf on top for 45–50 minutes.
- **3 and 4 Oven Aga,** cook on the 4th set of runners in the Baking Oven for 45–50 minutes.
- **Rayburn,** cook on the 5th set of runners in the Main Oven with the Thermodial reading Bake for 45–50 minutes.

Variations

Orange drizzle cake Replace lemon zest in cake with orange zest and lemon juice in topping with orange juice.

James says...

I don't know why poppy seeds are in this cake, but they make it look pretty.

angel cake.

A fat-free cake.

serves 8

185g caster sugar
60g plain flour
6 egg whites
Pinch salt
¾ tsp cream of tartar
2 drops vanilla essence

Here's how to make it...

- Preheat the oven to 180°C (160°C if using a fan oven) or Gas Mark 4.
- Sieve 100g of the caster sugar and all the flour together, do this three times to ensure the mixture gets plenty of air in and set aside.
- Whisk the egg whites with the salt and cream of tartar in a grease-free bowl until light and fluffy. Whisk through the last 85g caster sugar and vanilla.
- Fold though the sieved flour and sugar mixture.
- Pour into a ring-shaped tin measuring 18cm across the top and 7cm deep, or a 23cm cake tin.
- Bake for 20–25 minutes until the cake springs back when lightly pressed.
- Turn the tin upside down on a cooling tray and leave, the cake should fall out.
- **2 Oven Aga,** cook on the 4th set of runners in the Roasting Oven with the cold plain shelf on top for 20–25 minutes.
- **3 and 4 Oven Aga,** cook on the 4th set of runners in the Baking Oven for 20–25 minutes.
- **Rayburn,** cook on the 5th set of runners in the Main Oven with the Thermodial reading Bake for 20–25 minutes.

Variations

Almond angel cake Add 1 drop almond essence to cake mixture.

Chocolate angel cake Replace 1 tbsp plain flour with 1 tbsp cocoa powder.

James says...

As this cake is fat-free, it will freeze really well for up to three months.

gluten-free chocolate cake.

A wheat-free chocolate cake.

serves 4

6 eggs, separated
500g caster sugar
250g butter or margarine, softened
100g plain chocolate, melted with 125ml boiling water
1 tsp vanilla extract

500g rice flour
2 tbsp cornflour
1 tsp baking powder
1 tsp bicarbonate of soda
½ tsp salt
280ml buttermilk

Here's how to make it...

- Preheat the oven to 180°C (160°C if using a fan oven) or Gas Mark 4. Grease and line a 20cm spring form cake tin.
- Whisk the egg whites until frothy and then whisk in 125g of the sugar. Set aside.
- Cream the butter or margarine with the remaining sugar until the mixture is light and fluffy and drops off the end of a spoon to the count of two. Add egg yolks, chocolate and vanilla and beat well.
- Add all the other ingredients and mix well.
- Gently fold in the whisked egg whites.
- Pour into the prepared tin and bake for 30–35 minutes until a skewer comes out clean when inserted into the centre of the cake.

- **2 Oven Aga,** cook on the 4th set of runners in the Roasting Oven with the cold plain shelf on top for 30–35 minutes.
- **3 and 4 Oven Aga,** cook on the 4th set of runners in the Baking Oven for 30–35 minutes.
- **Rayburn,** cook on the 5th set of runners in the Main Oven with the Thermodial reading Bake for 30–35 minutes.

Variations

Gluten-free chocolate mocha cake Add 1 tbsp coffee extract to cake mix.

Gluten-free chocolate chilli cake Add 1 tsp mild chilli powder to cake mix.

Gluten-free cardamom chocolate cake Add 1 tsp ground cardamom seeds to cake.

James says...

Wheat, oats, barley and rye all contain a protein called gluten that some people are allergic to. Gluten is the elastic bit in flour that makes bread stretch. In this recipe we have used flours from different carbohydrates to replace the need for wheat flour.

egg-free apple, sultana and cinnamon cake.

A tasty moist cake.

serves 8

- 125g butter or margarine, softened
- 90g soft brown sugar
- 1 tsp bicarbonate of soda
- 1 tsp hot water
- 300g cooked apple purée
- 300g wholemeal self raising flour
- 180g chopped sultanas
- 1 tsp ground cinnamon
- 2 tbsp slivered almonds

Here's how to make it...

- Preheat the oven to 180°C (160°C if using a fan oven) or Gas Mark 4. Grease and line a 23cm cake tin.
- Cream the butter or margarine with the sugar until light and fluffy and the mixture falls off the end of a spoon to the count of two.
- Mix the bicarbonate of soda with water and add it to the butter mixture.
- Stir all the other ingredients, except the almonds, into the creamed mixture until combined.
- Pour the cake mixture into the prepared tin and decorate with almonds on top.
- Bake for 1 hour until set and golden, the cake has shrunk away from the sides and a skewer comes out clean when inserted. Cool on a wire rack.

- 🍃 **2 Oven Aga,** cook on the 4th set of runners in the Roasting Oven with the cold plain shelf on top for 1 hour.
- 🍃 **3 and 4 Oven Aga,** cook on the 4th set of runners in the Baking Oven for 1 hour.
- 🍃 **Rayburn,** cook on the 5th set of runners in the Main Oven with the Thermodial reading Bake for 1 hour.

Variations

Egg-free apple, date and walnut cake Replace sultanas with 60g chopped walnuts and 90g chopped dates.

James says...

This recipe uses wholemeal self raising flour. It's best not to sieve this type of flour as the bran will separate from the white flour and be left in the sieve.

chocolate chilli polenta cake.

Slightly grainy in texture, but very moist.

serves 8

150g self raising flour
75g polenta
50g ground almonds
125g butter or margarine, softened
125g caster sugar
2 eggs, lightly beaten
100g plain chocolate, melted
2 tsp vanilla extract
1 red chilli, finely chopped

Here's how to make it...

- Preheat the oven to 180°C (160°C if using a fan oven) or Gas Mark 4. Grease and line a 20cm cake tin.
- Mix the flour, polenta and ground almonds, set aside.
- Cream the butter or margarine and sugar together until light and fluffy and the mixture drops off a spoon to the count of two.
- Gradually add the eggs in three additions, beating well between each addition.
- Add the chocolate, vanilla and chilli. Mix well, add the flour mixture and mix through.
- Pour into the prepared tin.
- Bake for 1 hour until the cake comes away from the sides of the tin and a skewer comes out clean when inserted into the middle of the cake.

- **2 Oven Aga,** cook on the 4th set of runners in the Roasting Oven with the cold plain shelf on top for 1 hour.
- **3 and 4 Oven Aga,** cook on the 4th set of runners in the Baking Oven for 1 hour.
- **Rayburn,** cook on the 5th set of runners in the Main Oven with the Thermodial reading Bake for 1 hour.

Variations

Lemon polenta cake Replace the chocolate, vanilla and chilli with finely grated zest and juice of 1 lemon.

Marmalade polenta cake Replace the chocolate, vanilla and chilli with 150g marmalade.

James says...
Chocolate and chilli are a great combination. You can always use dried chillies instead of fresh.

lamingtons.

A traditional Australian cake. I first had them in Sydney. Such a great city.

serves 8

Cake mixture
3 eggs
150g caster sugar
200g self raising flour
50g cornflour
15g butter, melted
3 tbsp boiling water

Chocolate icing
500g icing sugar
75g cocoa
15g butter
150ml milk
500g desiccated coconut

Here's how to make it...

- Preheat the oven to 180°C (160°C if using a fan oven) or Gas Mark 4. Grease and line a 18 x 28cm cake tin.
- Whisk the eggs and sugar together until thick and creamy and you can make a shape in the mixture that sits for a few seconds.
- Gently fold in the flour and cornflour. Add the butter and water, fold through.
- Bake for 30–35 minutes until the cake is set and golden. Cool on a rack.
- To make the icing, sift icing sugar and cocoa into a heatproof bowl. Stir in butter and milk. Stir over a pan of boiling water until glossy.
- Trim the brown sides from the cake. Cut into 16 even sized pieces. Dip each side into chocolate icing and roll in coconut.

- 2 Oven Aga, cook on the 4th set of runners in the Roasting Oven with the cold plain shelf on top for 30–35 minutes.
- 3 and 4 Oven Aga, cook on the 4th set of runners in the Baking Oven for 30–35 minutes.
- Rayburn, cook on the 5th set of runners in the Main Oven with the Thermodial reading Bake for 30–35 minutes.

Variations

Jam Lamingtons Lamingtons can be cut in half and jam spread in the middle before covering in chocolate and coconut.

James says...
Lamingtons also make a good dessert. Serve with cream or ice-cream.

county armagh bramley apple cake.

County Armagh where I grew up is full of orchards, particularly those with Bramley apples. This cake makes the best of Bramley apples and produces a moreish moist cake.

serves 8

- 450g Bramley apples, peeled, cored and thinly sliced
- Grated rind and juice of 1 lemon
- 175g butter or margarine, softened
- 175g caster sugar
- 3 eggs, beaten
- 225g self raising flour
- ½ tsp baking powder
- ½ tsp ground cinnamon
- 5 tbsp raisins
- 2 tbsp chopped hazelnuts
- Dusting of icing sugar to decorate

Here's how to make it...

- Preheat the oven to 180°C (160°C if using a fan oven) or Gas Mark 4. Grease and line a 23cm cake tin. A spring form one is best for this recipe.
- Sprinkle the apples with lemon juice and set aside.
- Cream the butter or margarine, lemon rind and all but 1 tbsp of the sugar until light and fluffy. Beat in the eggs in three goes. Sift flour and baking powder together and fold into the creamed mixture.
- Spoon half of the mixture into the prepared cake tin. Arrange apple slices on top. Mix the remaining sugar with the cinnamon and sprinkle over apples. Scatter the raisins and hazelnuts over the apples.

- Bake for 1 hour, until the cake comes away from the sides of the tin and a skewer inserted comes out clean.
- Cool in the tin for 15 minutes, turn out and dust with icing sugar.
- 2 Oven Aga, cook on the 4th set of runners in the Roasting Oven with the cold plain shelf on top for 1 hour.
- 3 and 4 Oven Aga, cook on the 4th set of runners in the Baking Oven for 1 hour.
- Rayburn, cook on the 5th set of runners in the Main Oven with the Thermodial reading Bake for 1 hour.

Variations

Dorset apple cake Add 25g ground almonds when adding flour. Remove raisins and nuts. Cook in a greased and lined Swiss roll tin.

James says...

Bramley apples are best in this recipe as their texture holds the shape together well when cooking. Dessert apples may produce too much liquid when cooking and this can make for a soggy cake.

walnut and date cake.

Great with a cuppa.

makes 12 slices

100g stoned dates
grated rind of 1 orange
2 teabags
100ml boiling water
100g butter or margarine, softened
100g soft light brown sugar
2 eggs, lightly beaten
1 tbsp treacle
100g plain flour
1 tsp baking powder
½ tsp mixed spice
100g walnuts, chopped
100g raisins
10 walnut halves

Here's how to make it...

- Soak the dates, orange rind and teabags in the water overnight. Drain and dry the dates on kitchen paper, discard the teabags.
- Preheat the oven to 180°C (160°C if using a fan oven) or Gas Mark 4. Grease and line a 1kg loaf tin.
- Cream the butter or margarine and sugar until light and fluffy and the mixture drops off the end of a spoon to the count of two. Beat in the eggs in three stages. Add the treacle and mix well.
- Fold in all the other ingredients, except the walnut halves.
- Place the mixture into the prepared tin and place the walnut halves on top.
- Bake for 30–40 minutes until the cake comes away form the sides of the tin and a skewer comes out clean when inserted into the middle of the cake.

- **2 Oven Aga,** cook on the 4th set of runners in the Roasting Oven with the cold plain shelf on top for 35–40 minutes.
- **3 and 4 Oven Aga,** cook on the 4th set of runners in the Baking Oven for 35–40 minutes.
- **Rayburn,** cook on the 5th set of runners in the Main Oven with the Thermodial reading Bake for 35–40 minutes.

Variations

Walnut, date and coffee cake Add 1 tbsp coffee essence into mixture after adding eggs.

James says...

It's important to soak the dates so they soften and produce a better bite for the cake.

cherry and almond cake.

A delicious, traditional cake that freezes well.

serves 8

- 100g blanched almonds
- 200g butter or margarine, softened
- 225g golden caster sugar
- 3 eggs, beaten
- 200g self raising flour
- 225g glacé cherries, halved
- 55g flaked almonds

Here's how to make it...

- Preheat the oven to 180°C (160°C if using a fan oven) or Gas Mark 4. Grease and line a deep 20cm cake tin.
- Place the almonds on a baking tray and toast in the oven for 5 minutes. Tip them into a food processor and whizz until fine.
- Cream the butter and sugar together until light and fluffy and the mixture drops off the end of a spoon to the count of two. Add the eggs a bit at a time and mix together. Add the flour, cherries and ground almonds and pour into the tin. Place flaked almonds on top.
- Bake for 1 hour 10 minutes until the top is golden and a skewer comes out clean when inserted into the middle of the cake.
- 2 Oven Aga, cook on the 4th set of runners in the Roasting Oven with the cold plain shelf on top for 1 hour 10 minutes.
- 3 and 4 Oven Aga, cook on the 4th set of runners in the Baking Oven for 1 hour 10 minutes.
- Rayburn, cook on the 5th set of runners in the Main Oven with the Thermodial reading Bake for 1 hour 10 minutes.

Variations

Cherry and walnut cake Replace blanched almonds with 100g walnuts.

James says...
This recipe uses golden caster sugar. It's just a bit less refined than white caster sugar and gives cakes a lovely golden colour.

cake toppings.

cake.

buttercream. orange cream. lemon cream. coffee cream. chocolate cream. coloured cream. ganache. mocha ganache. chocolate orange ganache. american frosting. orange frosting. vanilla frosting. coffee frosting. lemon frosting. coloured frosting. chantilly cream. orange chantilly cream. mint chantilly cream. lemon chantilly cream. coffee chantilly cream.

butter cream.

Sweet and fluffy, it's a quick topping for cakes and can be coloured to be as pretty as you like.

covers a 20cm cake

150g icing sugar
100g butter, softened
½ tsp vanilla extract

Here's how to make it...

- Sieve the icing sugar into a mixing bowl.
- Add the butter and cream together with a wooden spoon until the mixture is soft and creamy in texture and white in colour. Add vanilla and mix through.

Variations

Orange cream Add a few drops of orange colouring and finely grated orange zest to butter and icing sugar.

Lemon cream Add a few drops of yellow colouring and finely grated lemon zest to butter and icing sugar.

Coffee cream Add 2 tsp instant coffee powder to icing sugar.

Chocolate cream Add 2 tbsp cocoa or drinking chocolate to icing sugar.

Coloured cream Add a few drops food colouring after creaming butter and icing sugar together and mix well.

James says...

Be sure to use icing sugar and not caster sugar as caster sugar makes a granular mix; icing sugar makes a smooth one.

ganache.

It's a gooey chocolate cake covering

covers a 20cm cake

125g plain or milk chocolate
125g whipping or double cream

Here's how to make it...

- Melt the chocolate in a bowl over a pan of simmering water.
- Remove from the heat and mix in the cream.
- Cool over iced water until the consistency of golden syrup.
- Pour over the cake and allow to set.

Variations

Mocha ganache Add 1 tbsp strong espresso coffee.

Chocolate orange ganache Add 1 tbsp Cointreau.

James says...

You can make the ganache in advance if you like. Put it in an airtight container, or cover well with clingfilm, and store in the fridge overnight. Warm through slightly before using, either in the microwave with great care not to overheat, or on the side of the Aga or Rayburn.

american frosting.

Makes a delicious cake covering that is crunchy on the outside and soft in the middle.

covers a 21cm cake

2 large egg whites
250g caster sugar
4 tbsp water

Here's how to make it...

- Place all the ingredients into a large bowl over a pan of boiling water.
- Whisk continuously for 12–15 minutes with an electric mixer until the mixture thickens and holds its shape.
- Spread quickly over the cake to produce a swirl pattern. Be quick as it will set quickly.

Variations

Orange frosting Add 1 tsp Cointreau or orange essence.

Vanilla frosting Add 1 tsp vanilla extract or seeds of 1 vanilla pod.

Coffee frosting Add 1 tbsp coffee essence.

Lemon frosting Add finely grated zest of one lemon.

Coloured frosting Add 1 tsp of any food colouring.

James says...

This recipe can be tricky – make sure you have your cake ready to ice as the frosting begins to set very quickly.

chantilly cream.

Crème Chantilly in French – it's very sweet and generally flavoured with vanilla.

covers a 21cm cake

300ml double or whipping cream
1 tbsp icing sugar

1 tsp vanilla extract or 2 tsp vanilla essence or seeds of 1 fresh vanilla pod

Here's how to make it...

- Place all the ingredients into a bowl and whisk (by hand or using a mixer) until light and fluffy.
- Place back into the refrigerator for 30 minutes before putting on top of cake.

Variations

Orange Chantilly cream Add 2–3 tsp Cointreau before whipping.

Mint Chantilly cream Add 2–3 tsp Crème de Menthe, before whipping.

Lemon Chantilly cream Add 2–3 tsp Limonchello before whipping.

Coffee Chantilly cream Add 2 tsp coffee essence before whipping.

James says...

Make sure the cream is well chilled before you start and that you don't whisk it for too long in case it turns to butter!

sponge – creamed mixture. sponge – whisked mixture. sponge – genoese. sponge – all in 1. victoria sandwich. chocolate beetroot cake. marshmallow cake. cola crater cake. carrot cake. parkin with apples. brownies. caraway cake. new york cheesecake. chilled cheesecake. rolo cake. mike's red velvet cake. rich fruit cake. saucepan cake. mexican chilli mocha cake. nectarine cake. madeira cake. genoa cake. ginger cake. gateau frazier. marble marshmallow spice cake with fudgy topping. caramel nut cake. pound cake. marmalade cake. chocolate fudge cake. alhambra. gateau pithiviers. cake in a cup. self saucing cake. rock cakes. breakfast loaf cake. malt loaf. pineapple upside-down cake. drizzle cake. angel cake. gluten-free chocolate cake. egg-free apple, sultana and cinnamon cake. chocolate chilli polenta cake. lamingtons. county armagh bramley apple cake. walnut and date cake. cherry and almond cake. butter cream. ganache. american frosting. chantilly cream.

index of recipes.

index of recipes

alhambra1	58
american frosting	90
coffee frosting	90
coloured frosting	90
lemon frosting	90
orange frosting	90
vanilla frosting	90
angel cake	71
almond angel cake	71
chocolate angel cake	71
breakfast loaf cake	65
mango figgy loaf	65
brownies	30
blondies	30
orange brownies	30
triple chocolate brownies	30
butter cream	88
chocolate cream	88
coffee cream	88
coloured cream	88
lemon cream	88
orange cream	88
cake in a cup	62
alcoholic syrup cake in a cup	62
chocolate cake in a cup	62
caraway cake	31
wholemeal caraway cake	31
caramel nut cake	52
hazelnut caramel cake	53
pecan caramel cake	53
carrot cake	26
carrot and pumpkin cake	27
courgette cake	27
chantilly cream	91
coffee chantilly cream	91
lemon chantilly cream	91
mint chantilly cream	91
orange chantilly cream	91
cherry and almond cake	84
cherry and walnut cake	85

chilled cheesecake	34
orange cheesecake	34
raspberry cheesecake	34
strawberry cheesecake	34
chocolate beetroot cake	20
chocolate, orange and beetroot cake	21
chocolate, raspberry and beetroot cake	21
mocca chocolate and beetroot cake	21
chocolate chilli polenta cake	76
lemon polenta cake	77
marmalade polenta cake	77
chocolate fudge cake	56
chocolate cherry fudge cake	57
chocolate orange fudge cake	57
chocolate icing	78
cola crater cake	24
coffee cola cake	25
coffee fudge icing	50
county armagh bramley apple cake	80
dorset apple cake	81
cream cheese topping	32
crème mousseline	48
drizzle cake	70
orange drizzle cake	70
drizzle topping	70
egg-free apple, sultana and cinnamon cake	74
egg-free apple, date and walnut cake	75
fudge icing	52
fudge topping	56
ganache	89
chocolate orange ganache	89
mocca ganache	89
gateau frazier	48

Entry	Page
gateau pithiviers	60
apple pithiviers	61
pear pithiviers	61
genoa cake	46
ginger cake	47
treacle cake	47
gluten-free chocolate cake	72
gluten-free cardamom chocolate cake	73
gluten-free chocolate chilli cake	73
gluten-free chocolate mocca cake	73
lamingtons	78
jam lamingtons	79
madeira cake	44
almond madeira cake	45
cherry madeira cake	45
coffee and walnut madeira cake	45
dundee cake	45
ginger madeira cake	45
malt loaf	66
date malt loaf	67
marble marshmallow spice cake with fudgy topping	50
marmalade cake	55
marmalade and almond cake	55
marshmallow cake	22
chocolate marshmallow cake	23
mexican chilli mocca cake	40
mexican caraway mocca cake	41
mike's red velvet cake	36
beetroot red velvet cake	37
devil's food cake	37
nectarine cake	42
peach cake	43
plum cake	43
new york cheesecake	32
blueberry new york cheesecake	33
raspberry new york cheesecake	33
strawberry new york cheesecake	33
toffee new york cheesecake	33
parkin with apples	28
treacle parkin	29
pineapple upside-down cake	68
pear upside-down cake	69
pound cake	54
chocolate pound cake	54
citrus pound cake	54
rich fruit cake	38
rock cakes	64
cherry rock cakes	64
chocolate rock cakes	64
rolo cake	35
rolo orange cake	35
saucepan cake	39
cherry cake in a saucepan	39
quick dundee cake	39
self saucing cake	63
chocolate self saucing cake	63
sponge – all in 1	17
almond sponge – all in 1	17
chocolate sponge – all in 1	17
coffee sponge – all in 1	17
lemon sponge – all in 1	17
sponge – creamed mixture	12
almond sponge – creamed mixture	13
chocolate sponge – creamed mixture	13
coffee sponge – creamed mixture	13
lemon sponge – creamed mixture	13
sponge – genoese	16
almond sponge – genoese	16
chocolate sponge – genoese	16
coffee sponge – genoese	16
lemon sponge – genoese	16
sponge – whisked mixture	14
almond sponge – whisked mixture	15
chocolate sponge – whisked mixture	15
coffee sponge – whisked mixture	15
lemon sponge – whisked mixture	15
victoria sandwich	18
chocolate victoria sandwich	19
lemon victoria sandwich	19
walnut and date cake	82
walnut, date and coffee cake	83

Other books by James

2008 International Gourmand winner – Best Series of Food Books in the World

mix.

mix. is a comprehensive guide to basic proportions in cookery, giving the quantities needed for simple, everyday family food. Containing over 180 recipes, from how to make a white sauce to how to prepare pastry, this is an essential cookery book you will turn to again and again.

dinner.

dinner. is a book full of 50 recipes with variations to give over 120 family meal solutions at an everyday price, providing nutritious, good wholesome family food. dinner. saves money on food and fuel bills.

veg.

veg. gives clear, concise instructions for making family vegetarian dinners and exciting vegetable meal accompaniments using James' ethos: 'no fiddle, no fuss, just food'. Whether you grow your own vegetables, visit the greengrocer, shop at the market or buy them from a box scheme, veg. is a great book for you.